GW00702927

LITTLE BOOK OF THE
ASHES

By **Ralph Dellor and Stephen Lamb**

LITTLE BOOK OF THE
ASHES

This edition first published in the UK in 2009
By Green Umbrella Publishing

© Green Umbrella Publishing 2009

www.gupublishing.co.uk

Publishers Jules Gammond and Vanessa Gardner

Printed and bound in Poland

ISBN: 978-1-906635-46-6

Contents

Birth Of The Urn
1877–1883

Was it a ball, was it a bail or was it even a veil? That is the debate that has endured since 1882 when the famous Ashes urn came into existence. What exactly was it that was incinerated and put in the receptacle that has become one of sport's most exotic and revered trophies? In fact, the Ashes urn never has been a trophy as such, for it is only the concept of the Ashes that has gone to the victor. The artefact itself never has, although in recent times a replica has been presented, as has a large Waterford Crystal representation of the urn itself.

The existence of the Ashes was no more than notional until they took on a physical existence in 1882. Matches between the two countries began on March 15th, 1877 in Melbourne. The Australian captain Dave Gregory won the toss and decided to bat, so England's Alfred Shaw bowled the first ball in Test cricket to Charles Bannerman, who went on to become the first batsman to record a Test century. Allen Hill took the first Test wicket when he bowled Nat Thomson and held the first Test catch, to dismiss Tom Horan off the bowling of Shaw. Australia's Billy Midwinter (who was later to represent England) took the first five-wicket haul (5-78 off 54 four-ball overs), and John Blackham the first stumping, in England's second innings. Remarkably James Southerton, who was 49 years and 110 days old when the game began, remains the oldest Test debutant and was also the first Test cricketer to die, a mere three years later.

Thanks largely to Bannerman's 165

◀ The urn containing the coveted "ashes".

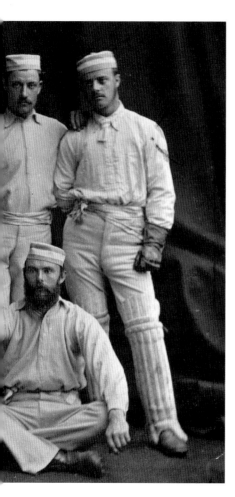

before he retired due to injury, Australia reached 245 all out in their first innings. England replied with 196 before Australia scored 104 in their second innings, with Shaw taking 5-38. This set the tourists a target of 154 to win, but Tom Kendall, ironically born in Bedford, took 7-55 to bowl England out for 108, leaving Australia winners by 45 runs. It was an amazing coincidence that exactly 100 years later, in a match on the same ground to celebrate the centenary of the first Test, the result was precisely the same. Australia won by 45 runs.

Back in 1877 England avenged their defeat, again at the MCG, the following month, in a match that featured another famous debutant, Frederick Spofforth, who was to dominate the match of 1882 that led directly to the conception of the Ashes. This parity between the two cricketing nations continued. Australia won the Test at Melbourne in January 1879; England won when Australia appeared at the Kennington Oval in 1880. Sydney became the third Test venue in cricket's history when four matches were played in 1881/82, with Australia winning two while two were drawn.

It was at the Oval in 1882 that the pattern of home superiority was broken.

◀ The first official Australian cricket team to visit England.

▶ A newspaper obituary on the death of English cricket which appeared after England lost the 1882 Test match against Australia.

Billy Murdoch won the toss for Australia and decided to bat, but the left arm medium pace of Lancashire's Dick Barlow proved too much for the visiting batsmen. Barlow took five for 19 as Australia were bowled out for 63, although they occupied the crease for 80 overs. Spofforth responded by taking seven for 46 as England took a first innings lead of 38. With the exception of Hugh Massie, who recorded his highest Test score of 55, Australia fared little better in their second innings to be all out for 122, leaving England to score 85 to win.

W.G. Grace opened with Albert "Monkey" Hornby, the England captain. Grace remained to score 32 and, at 53 for three, England were on course to secure the victory. But then Grace went. The fifth wicket fell with 66 on the board and 19 runs still needed, but Charles Studd, one of the leading batsmen of the day, had been held back in the order to counter any crisis in the lower order. That crisis became vividly apparent when the scoreboard showed 75 for eight. Spofforth was bowling superbly, but with only 10 runs to win and Studd striding to the wicket, the tension would surely be swept away. It was not. One spectator is reported to have died of a heart attack brought on by the excitement that caused another, reputedly, to gnaw

through the handle of his umbrella.

Studd's arrival came too late to influence the outcome. During the five minutes he batted, he did not face a single ball. Billy Barnes was caught off his glove before last man Ted Peate was bowled by Harry Boyle, and England were all out for 77 to lose by seven runs. For the first time (but certainly not the last!), the England cricket team became the subject of ridicule. As ever, the press turned to black humour to convey the national sentiment, with *Cricket – a Weekly Record of the Game* first off the mark on 31st August with a notice that read: "Sacred to the memory of England's supremacy in the cricket field which expired on the 29th day of August at The Oval. The end was Peate."

It was two days later that the famous mock obituary appeared in the *Sporting Times* (see image on right).

It was the reference to the ashes being taken to Australia that sparked the whole sequence of events that produced the little urn. It was also a clever choice of words, reflecting the public debate being conducted at the time over the legality or otherwise of cremation. Woking's Crematorium, the first in the country, was founded in 1878, when a piece of land close to St John's Village was bought by

In Affectionate Remembrance

OF

ENGLISH CRICKET,

WHICH DIED AT THE OVAL

ON

29th AUGUST, 1882,

Deeply lamented by a large circle of sorrowing friends and acquaintances.

R.I.P.

N.B.—The body will be cremated and the ashes taken to Australia.

▲ Frederick Spofforth.

It was the home of Sir William Clarke, a wealthy landowner who was returning to Victoria with his second wife, Lady Janet, aboard the P&O steamship *Peshawur*. Travelling from Gravesend with the Clarkes was the England team, led by the Hon. Ivo Bligh. Many years later, while England teams still travelled by ship to Australia, P&O was the chosen line and Tilbury was the port of departure – directly across the Thames from Gravesend.

A month after embarking from England, the *Peshawur* reached Colombo, where Bligh's team played against 18 locals and then a match against the Royal Dublin Fusiliers, before departing again for Adelaide. However, shortly after setting sail, the ship was in collision and had to return to port for repairs. She was five days late arriving in Adelaide, where another fixture was completed, before continuing to Melbourne where the team arrived exactly two months after leaving Gravesend.

Sir Henry Thompson, surgeon to Queen Victoria and founder of The Cremation Society in 1874. The story of the Ashes could therefore be said to go all the way from St. John's Village to St. John's Wood!

There is a detour in the story covering some 12,000 miles to Rupertswood – a stately home at Sunbury, near Melbourne.

In Melbourne, as everywhere else on the tour, the England team were lavishly feted, with Bligh responding to a toast by saying that he intended "to recover those ashes." Two weeks after arriving, the eight amateurs in the touring party were invited to Rupertswood, where Sir William had just learned that he was the first Australian

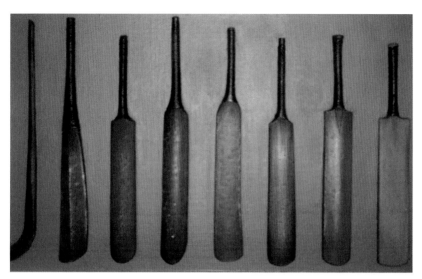

◀ A selection of historical cricket bats.

to be granted a hereditary title by Queen Victoria. The four professionals remained in Melbourne. At a dinner given in honour of the Australian team that had just returned from their tour of England, the captain, Billy Murdoch, gave a speech in which he too referred to the still mythical ashes, picking up on what Bligh had said earlier.

It was on this visit to Rupertswood that Bligh first met Florence Rose Murphy, the music tutor to Lady Clarke's children. Miss Murphy was not of noble birth, but despite the importance of social status at

the time, Bligh, later to become the 8th Earl of Darnley, was so taken with the lady that he decided that she would become his wife, no matter about the class divide. Bligh was suffering from one of the more unusual injuries to befall a cricketer at the time. His arm was in a sling after it was damaged during a tug-of-war on board the *Peshawur*. When a further injury, this time to his finger, befell him during a match in Melbourne, it was Florence Murphy who played Florence Nightingale to attend him.

Bligh and his amateur colleagues

returned to Rupertswood for Christmas, and it was then that the now celebrated urn took its important place in the history of cricket. There was no great planning, no elaborate ceremony. It was a spontaneous act dreamed up by Lady Janet, Florence Murphy and the other ladies of the house party while Bligh and his colleagues played a game against a local team comprising estate workers in the main, on Christmas Eve. According to a leading researcher into the origin of the Ashes at Rupertswood, Joy Munns, one of those estate workers, actually saw a bail being burnt at Lady Clarke's behest. She took the small pottery urn, perhaps from her dressing room, put the ashes of the bail in it and presented it to Bligh as a personal gift to mark his visit to Rupertswood, almost as a light-hearted gesture.

The estate worker, Pat Lyons, was in no doubt about the origin. He made no mention of a ball or a veil, but others suggested that it was after the third Test that a bail from the match was burned and put in the urn. There was also a tale that a housemaid at Cobham Hall in Kent, the home of the Darnleys, was one day dusting a mantleshelf and knocked the urn down into the fireplace, spilling the contents as it fell. In a panic, she dusted up some

◀ The Hon Ivo Bligh, captain of the first ever winning Ashes team.

◀◀ W.G. Grace.

ashes from the fireplace, put them in the urn and restored it to its rightful place as if nothing had happened. When the urn was later examined and then restored, cracks were found consistent with a fall, but the MCC committee at the time decided against analysing the contents. Better to let romantic folklore prevail than discover that the urn is filled with the remains of a bag of nutty slack!

The fact that the urn remained at Cobham Hall until 1929 is proof that it was always regarded as a personal possession rather than a trophy. It was only when Lord Darnley died in 1927, having realised the wider significance of the little urn to the cricketing world, that Lady Darnley decided to honour her late husband's wishes by

donating it to the MCC. It was displayed in the Long Room at Lord's until the opening of the ground's museum in 1953.

Just as there is controversy over the content of the urn, so there was about the first series of its existence as a cricketing object. The first Test was played at Melbourne as a timeless match, starting on December 30th, 1882. New Year's Eve was deemed to be a rest day, and the match was completed by January 2nd. Batting first, Australia made 291, but England could manage only 177 in reply. In those days a lead of 114 was enough for Australia to enforce the follow on, and batting a second time England set them a target of only 56 to win. Australia attained it with just one wicket down.

The second Test began on January 19th, again at Melbourne and was again completed in three days, but this time with the result reversed. Australia replied to England's 294 with 114, and following on were bowled out for 153 to lose by an innings and 27 runs. Billy Bates became the first man to take a Test hat-trick in the first innings when he took seven wickets in total, and he claimed seven more in Australia's second knock. This match was affected by the weather, as was the third Test in Sydney. This time England took a

◀ Rupertswood, birthplace of the Ashes.

first innings lead of a mere 29 runs before setting Australia a target of 153. They were bowled out for 83 to seal England's victory by 69 runs.

That should have been the end of the series, scheduled for three matches. However, the English party agreed to play a fourth match at Sydney, as it was thought that England had enjoyed the better conditions in the second and third matches. The first three had been between England and the Australian team that had toured England in 1882. The fourth match was against a side for which all Australians were eligible for selection. There was also an agreement, born of mysterious logic, that the four innings would be played on four separate pitches.

Australia won by four wickets, and this was merely the first, but not the last instance of matches between the two countries falling outside the compass of the Ashes. As the series was scheduled to be decided over three games, historians regard the fourth match as no more than a one-off. *Wisden* has recorded it as such, and it is difficult to argue with what might be termed the game's official record. To add further intrigue, Bligh himself considered that the series had been drawn 2-2, referring to that score line in a farewell speech at the Melbourne Cricket Club.

Wisden is not alone in thinking otherwise. At the conclusion of the third Test, a poem was published in the *Melbourne Punch* suggesting that Australia had lost the series and the Ashes were regained by England. When Bligh returned to Rupertswood prior to his departure for home, Lady Clarke fixed a hand-written verse from the *Melbourne Punch* poem to the urn, where it remains to this day. It reads:

> *"When Ivo goes back with*
> *the urn, the urn;*
> *Studds, Steel, Read and Tylecote*
> *return, return,*
> *The welkin will ring loud,*
> *The great crowd will feel proud,*
> *Seeing Barlow and Bates with*
> *the urn, the urn;*
> *And the rest coming home with*
> *the urn."*

It is a verse unlikely to win any poetry prizes, yet it suggests that the urn might have been brandished to the crowd as a trophy. It was not, and by the time it was felt necessary to have such a trophy, age had taken its toll on an increasingly fragile piece of pottery that had come to symbolise the most revered contest in cricket.

◀ Billy Murdoch who captained the Australian team on early tours to England.

The Golden Age
1884-1914

England's grip on the urn was consolidated in the 1884 series thanks to a solitary win, by an innings and five runs, in the first ever Test match at Lord's. After Allan Steel made 148, George Ulyett bowled at his quickest on a deteriorating pitch to take seven for 36, including a return catch off the hard-hitting George Bonnor that left his team-mates awestruck. In the subsequent encounter at the Oval, Australia racked up 551 on a dry pitch in bright sunshine, their esteemed captain Billy Murdoch leading the way with the first ever Test double century and every England player bowled. Remarkably the most successful was their wicket-keeper Alfred Lyttelton, who handed the gloves to W.G. Grace before polishing off the Australian tail with lobs, recording figures

◀ Part of the wall surrounding cricket's most famous ground.

◀◀ George Ulyett (second row, second from left) in a Yorkshire CCC team Photo.

of four for 19 from his 12 overs. One of his wickets was that of Bill Midwinter, caught by Grace. England were forced to follow on despite a remarkable century from Walter Read, batting at number 10, but held out for a draw, concluding a tightly-contested series between two evenly-matched teams.

Financial wrangling prevented Australia from fielding their strongest team in every game of the 1884/85 series, which took some of the gloss off England's 3-2 win. Bobby Peel was England's bowling hero, finishing the tour with an astonishing haul

of over 300 wickets in all matches played with his slow left arm bowling, while the rather quicker Billy Barnes was another key influence on the Test series. The third Test at Sydney produced one of the great Ashes finishes, when Spofforth was handed the ball with England needing just seven runs for victory and one wicket remaining. His first ball was a fast, lifting delivery that Wilf Flowers, on 56 at the time, could only push to Edwin Evans at point.

Financial disputes, combined with key retirements, were to dog Australia

for the rest of the decade. Tup Scott's much-heralded 1886 team in England was to be at the wrong end of the first ever Ashes whitewash. Bad weather dogged the Australians through May, and in June the great Spofforth was forced out of action for a month by a hand injury. They competed well in the first Test at Old Trafford, which England won by four wickets thanks to a magnificent all-round performance by Dick Barlow. But at Lord's, England were rampant thanks to Arthur Shrewsbury, whose 164 beat the record individual Ashes score held by Grace. The Champion was not to be eclipsed for long; in the next game at the Oval he reclaimed the record at the first opportunity with his Test-best score of 170. England won both matches by an innings.

Their run continued in 1886/87, as Australia's weakened batting line-up proved easy prey for George Lohmann, Barnes and Peel. But a remarkable feature of both the Tests was the emergence of Charlie Turner and John Ferris, a right-left arm combination that accounted for 35 England wickets in the two matches. Their efforts could not prevent another defeat in the one-off Test in Sydney the following season, in which Peel and Lohmann took nine wickets each.

Turner and Ferris tasted victory at last

at Lord's in 1888, with 18 wickets between them on a damp pitch. But England, now led by Grace, struck back to such effect that Australia failed to muster 100 in three of their next four innings. Peel, Barnes and Johnny Briggs were their tormentors at the Oval, and Grace made the game's top score of 38 on a damp pitch at Old Trafford before Peel bowled England to an innings victory that secured the rubber. But signs of an Australian revival were apparent in 1890. Grace saw England to a seven-wicket win at Lord's, in a match that was a wicket-keeping triumph in that neither the experienced John Blackham of Australia nor the England debutant, Gregor MacGregor, conceded a bye throughout. There were shades of 1882 at the Oval as England, set 95 to win, squeaked home by just two wickets. The first of only three total Ashes washouts followed at Old Trafford.

Influential though Grace had been in England over this period, his visit to Australia in 1891/92 was the first for 18 years, and he witnessed confirmation of a revival in Australian fortunes. The bowling of Turner and the all-rounder George Giffen, the latter an intermittent presence hitherto, helped Australia to successive wins which regained the Ashes after nine years. Their batting line-up was greatly

◀ Bobby Peel, one of the finest bowlers of the 1890s.

▲ The great bowler George Lohmann.

with Giffen and Syd Gregory to the fore, amassed 586. England were forced to follow on, but showed such resilience all the way down the order that Australia were set a victory target of 177. They were within 64 with eight wickets in hand by the fifth evening (Tests were timeless in this series), but heavy overnight rain resulted in a sticky wicket. Peel and Briggs cleaned Australia up, and for the first of only two occasions in Ashes history, the team following on had won.

The fast bowling heroics of Tom Richardson combined with a captain's 173 from Andrew Stoddart to put England two up at Melbourne, but the all-round form of Albert Trott then helped Australia to level the series with one to play. 100,000 people converged on Melbourne to watch the decider, won by England on a perfect wicket on day five, spurred on by a chanceless 140 from the Yorkshireman Jack Brown.

Another close encounter followed in England in 1896, with England prevailing at Lord's after Richardson had reduced a youthful Australia to 53 all out in their first innings. The tourists levelled things at Old Trafford with a three-wicket win after England, the efforts of their debutant Indian prince K.S. Ranjitsinhji notwithstanding, were again forced to follow on. The

strengthened by Alec Bannerman and John Lyons, although the urn returned to England a year later thanks to a solitary win by an innings at the Oval.

The rubber played in Australia in 1894/95 remains one of the most engaging of all time. It began with an astonishing turnaround in Sydney, after Australia,

◀ Andrew Stoddart, who was the Wisden Cricketer of the Year 1893.

decider at the Oval was played on a rain-ruined wicket, and although England won it by 66 runs after dismissing Australia for just 44 in their second innings, it was plain that their supremacy was under threat.

So it proved 18 months later, as a new generation of batsmen, notably Joe Darling and Clem Hill, turned the heat of an unusually hot Australian summer on England's bowlers, after the tourists won the opening encounter in Sydney. All four of the remaining matches went to Australia, whose attack of Ernie Jones, Monty Noble, Trott and Bill Howell covered all bases. They were on a roll, which continued on their next visit in 1899. England were outplayed in the first Test at Trent Bridge, where a rearguard 93 from Ranjitsinhji saved them, but were annihilated at Lord's after both Hill and an emerging legend, Victor Trumper, scored 135. It was to be the only result of a hard-fought series.

Remarkably, the succession of results in the 1901/02 rubber was identical to that four years earlier. How it might have ended if Sydney Barnes, one of the great bowlers of all time, had not been injured after taking 19 wickets in two Tests is a matter for conjecture. His wickets in Melbourne could not prevent Australia from levelling the series after the opening defeat, after which Noble and Hugh Trumble tormented England's batsmen, with the notable exception of their captain, Archie MacLaren. Barnes's tour ended in the third Test at Adelaide, which Australia eventually won by four wickets on the sixth day. They took two fewer to win the fourth back in Sydney, and just three on a rain-affected pitch at the MCG, wrapping up the series 4-1.

Rain was the overriding influence at Edgbaston just three months later, favouring England on day two as Wilfred Rhodes and George Hirst skittled the Aussies for just 36 in reply to England's 376. Thy followed on and but for 12 hours of incessant rain England would surely have won the game. A flu-ridden Australian camp were probably relieved by the rain which forced a further abandonment at Lord's, allowing Trumble, still Australia's foremost bowler, further recovery time from injury. With Noble, he played a key role in Australia's 143-run win in the only Test match ever to be played at Bramall Lane in Sheffield.

Two classic contests followed. At Old Trafford, Trumper and Stanley Jackson traded centuries to leave things close to parity at the halfway stage, but Australia were then dismissed for 86, leaving England just 124 to win. Despite overnight rain, at

68 for one they were coasting, but brilliant bowling by Trumble and Jack Saunders reduced them to 116 for nine. In came last man Fred Tate, who after edging Saunders to the leg-side boundary, was memorably bowled by a shooter to give Australia a three-run win, ensuring their retention of the urn. It was a sad end for Tate in his

◀ Australian cricketer Albert Trott.

▼ Ranjitsinhji, one of the greatest batsmen of his time.

only Test, and he was reputed to have sat in the dressing room in the aftermath musing that he had a lad at home who would one day avenge him. Maurice Tate was to do just that. The Oval encounter ended amid similar tension, but after an eye-catching century by Gilbert Jessop, England held their nerve despite losing their ninth wicket with 15 still needed, thanks to a famous last-ditch stand between Hirst and Rhodes.

Such heroics notwithstanding, England had now lost four Ashes series in as many years, and Pelham Warner's team headed Down Under in 1903 with national honour at stake. A remarkable innings of 287 by Reginald "Tip" Foster, one of seven brothers to play first-class cricket, remains the highest score by a Test debutant and the highest for England in Australia. It provided the foundation for a five-wicket win at the SCG, and rain helped England go two up in Melbourne, damaging the wicket after they had scored 221 runs on the first day. Rhodes took 15 wickets in the match, then a Test record, and would have had more but for abysmal England fielding which resulted in eight catches being dropped off him.

Trumper's batting bravado could not save Australia in that game, but helped win the next one in Adelaide, along with the bowling of Trumble and Bert

Hopkins. By now though, England had deployed the inventor of the googly, B.J.T. Bosanquet, and it was his wizardry that secured victory back in Sydney, regaining the Ashes for England. Victory on a sticky MCG wicket in the final game was scant consolation for Australia.

Bosanquet was again influential in 1905, although the all-round performance of Jackson, now England's captain, was a bigger reason for their Ashes retention. His predecessor, MacLaren, scored a masterly 140 at Trent Bridge before Bosanquet span his way through Australia in the gloom to put England one up. After draws at Lord's and Headingley, Australia were again unstitched by rain at Old Trafford, which livened up the pitch after the hosts had posted 446. The fast bowler Walter Brearley took eight wickets as Australia were routed by an innings and 80 runs. Big hundreds for C.B. Fry and Reggie Duff featured in the "dead" final Test at the Oval.

In 1907/08 England paid the penalty for not sending a fully representative team, and Australia regained the urn with a flourish. Their lower-order batsmen held their nerve to win a tight first Test in Sydney by two wickets, as did England's at Melbourne to win by an even smaller margin. Thereafter Australia were simply too strong, with

◀ Gilbert Jessop, one of the most exciting batsmen of his generation.

Clem Hill, batting at number nine because of flu, contributing 160 at Adelaide before England were bowled out by the two Jacks, Saunders and O'Connor. The duo prevailed again back at the MCG after a century from Warwick Armstrong had given Australia ballast, and another magnificent hundred from Trumper sealed the rubber by 4-1.

The young Jack Hobbs, who had made 83 in England's solitary win at Melbourne, took his team to an opening win in 1909 after Hirst and Colin Blythe got amongst Australia on a damp Edgbaston pitch. But it was to be England's only victory of the summer. At Lord's, an unbeaten 143 from Vernon Ransford gave the tourists a lead before Armstrong ripped through England with his leg breaks, and 1-1 became 2-1 at Headingley when England, after battling well on the first two days, were dismissed for just 87 on day three by the pace of Tibby Cotter and the spin of Charles Macartney. Eight wickets for Frank Laver featured in the Manchester draw, and stalemate was also the outcome at the Oval, where Australia's Warren Bardsley became the first man to score a century in each innings of a Test match.

England had now beaten Australia just twice in 10 Tests, and the mood was not

◀ Fielders surround the batsman on the damp Edgbaston pitch in 1909.

brightened by the first Ashes encounter of their 1911/12 tour. After losing their estimable captain, Pelham Warner, to illness, they also lost at Sydney, undone by the leg breaks and googlies of Herbert "Ranji" Hordern. But at Melbourne it was a bowling partnership – the now legendary right arm left arm pairing of Barnes and Frank Foster – which not only restored parity but set the tone for the series. On a perfect pitch, Barnes produced one of the spells of his life, taking five for six in 11 overs to reduce Australia to 38 for six. Although they recovered to reach 182, a Jack Hearne century helped the tourists to a lead, and Hobbs also reached three figures in the second innings to ensure an eight-wicket win.

Hobbs, not yet aged 21, continued his magnificent form with 187 at Adelaide as England passed 500 after Barnes and Foster had skittled Australia for 133, and although the hosts fought more doughtily in their second innings, England won by seven wickets. The bowling duo again mastered Australia back at the MCG, after Warner's replacement, Johnny Douglas, had put them in on a damp wicket. With Australia out for 191 and batting conditions much improved, Hobbs and Rhodes produced a record-breaking opening partnership that

put the Ashes firmly back in England's grasp. The total had reached 323 by the time Hobbs was dismissed for 178, and Rhodes followed for 179. Five wickets for Douglas then sealed Australia's fate by an innings and 225 runs. Even another 10-wicket haul for Hordern could not deny a rampant England back at the SCG, where the great Kent left-hander Frank Woolley excelled with 133.

Disharmony within the Australian ranks resulted in the absence of Trumper, Hill, Cotter, Armstrong and Ransford from the team that took part in a triangular series in England, also involving a weak South African side, in 1912. South Africa were beaten by Australia and trounced by England, before rain ruined the Ashes Tests at Lord's and Old Trafford. It also influenced the final Test at the Oval, where it took seven days for England to win on a sticky wicket. Hobbs and Woolley helped them to 245, and the latter then took five wickets in each innings as Australia's batsmen failed to master the conditions. As a series it did not hold a candle to its predecessor, and its significance was further diminished by the horrors that were to follow on the Western Front and Gallipoli over the ensuing years.

◀ Pelham Warner – a fine batsman and shrewd captain.

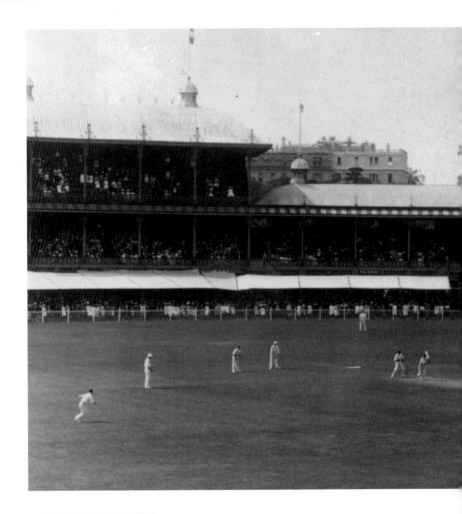

◄ The Melbourne Cricket Ground during the 1912 Test match.

Between The Wars

1918-1938

Such was the impact of the Great War, it was not until 1920-21 that activities between England and Australia resumed on the cricket field. The terrible slaughter meant that it was somehow inappropriate to try to conjure up the intensity of an Ashes battle any sooner. Both countries had suffered losses during the war as 34 first-class cricketers lost their lives, while age had called time on a number of Test careers. Above all, W.G. Grace had died in 1915, having first, reportedly, shaken his fist at zeppelins as they flew over his south London home. The Grand Old Man was defiant to the end.

It was therefore not surprising so many players were making their Test debuts when England and Australia took to the field at Sydney for the first time after the war in

December 1920. Johnny Douglas captained England while Warwick Armstrong led Australia, for whom Herbie Collins, Jack Gregory, Arthur Mailey, Bertie Oldfield, Nip Pellew, Jack Ryder and Johnny Taylor were all wearing a baggy green cap for the first time. By contrast, England had four men on Test debut – Patsy Hendren, Cecil Parkin, Jack Russell and Abe Waddington.

Australia triumphed by 377 runs in that match, and won the second Test in Melbourne by an innings and 91 runs. The margin in Adelaide was 119 runs, eight wickets in Melbourne again, and nine wickets back in Sydney. Australia won all five matches to secure an Ashes series for the first time since 1909, while inflicting a whitewash on England for the first time ever. England could boast some of the great names of cricket – Jack Hobbs, Frank Woolley and Wilfred Rhodes to name but three – but Armstrong's Australians were to become rated as one of the best sides ever to take the field, as was evident when the "Big Ship", as the physically imposing Armstrong was known, took his men to England in 1921.

England had not won a Test against Australia since August 1912, and were defeated in the first three of the 1921 series by margins of 10 wickets, eight wickets

and 219 runs. They even changed their captain after the second Test, with the Hon. Lionel Tennyson taking over from Douglas. England's batting and fielding were way below par, while Australia could boast batsmen like Warren Bardsley and Charles Macartney, and had as good a pair of fast bowlers as yet seen in the Test arena, Gregory and Ted McDonald.

All that impeded their triumphal march was the rain at Old Trafford that consigned the fourth Test to a draw with less than 250 overs possible. But in that short time there were two noteworthy incidents. The first came when England had reached 341 for four on the second day, (the first having been washed out – a decision that almost resulted in a riot by the crowd who had paid to get into the ground when there was little prospect of play). According to the Laws at the time, with the first day of three abandoned, it became a two-day match and no declaration could be made later than 100 minutes before the scheduled close of play. Tennyson went on to the field to declare, as was the practice then, with only 40 minutes remaining. The Australians knew of the ruling and stayed out on the field for a while before going off for a discussion, which resulted in England continuing their innings until close of play. In all the

◀ Johnny Douglas leading his team on to the field, 1921.

▶ The famous Kennington Oval was staging the final Test of the summer as early as 1926.

commotion it was forgotten that Armstrong had bowled the over immediately before the interruption, and he proceeded to bowl the one straight after the restart.

England were 231 runs in front with nine second innings wickets standing when the match ended. In the final Test at the Oval, England led by 258 runs with eight second innings wickets in hand when the three-day match ended as a draw. The progress of Armstrong's side throughout the land had been imperious. The Ashes were safely retained and he left a legacy that was eagerly taken up by Herbie Collins for the 1924/25 rubber.

The first Test in that series began in Sydney on December 19th and did not reach its conclusion until the 27th, with Christmas Day as the rest day. Timeless Tests were played throughout, with the first three matches going to seven days and the final two to five. Australia won the first, second and fifth Tests comfortably and the third narrowly, by just 11 runs. England at last ended the barren run that they had begun in 1912 and endured through 13 Tests by winning in Melbourne. The margin was as handsome as the victory was welcome – an innings and 29 runs.

When Australia visited England in 1926, rain and the dominance of bat over ball

◤ Don Bradman
adding to his
prolific batting
record at
Headingley.

resulted in the first four matches ending as draws. In a wet summer, the return to three-day Test matches was not conducive to positive results. However a timeless Test was scheduled for the Oval, and in four days England won a fascinating contest by 289 runs after dispensing with the services of Arthur Carr as captain and turning to the more flamboyant yet inexperienced Percy Chapman. It was not until Australia's second innings that England gained the ascendancy, built on the excellent batting of Hobbs and Herbert Sutcliffe, who opened the second innings with a partnership of 172 in difficult conditions. It had rained heavily the previous evening and the uncovered pitch was providing a true test of batting technique. *Wisden* recalls that "Richardson, while making the ball turn and rise quickly, stuck doggedly to the leg theory." A foretaste of six years hence!

Chapman took England to Australia in 1928/29, winning by a margin of 4-1 despite the appearance of a certain D.G. Bradman in the Australian side for the first Test in Brisbane. He was not a great success and was dropped for the Sydney Test before a recall at Melbourne resulted in innings of 79 and 112. But Wally Hammond made a superb double hundred for England (his second in consecutive

matches) to negate Bradman's efforts, and steered England to a 4-0 lead in Adelaide with another hundred. Australia won the "dead" match in Melbourne, with Bradman scoring his first match-winning hundred. There would be many more to follow.

The next came at Lord's in 1930 when he scored 254, having made 131 in a losing cause at Trent Bridge. It was at Headingley in the third Test that Bradman re-wrote the record books with an innings of 334. He failed at Old Trafford but secured the Ashes for Australia with 232 at the Oval in a victory by an innings and 39 runs. Bradman did not win the series for Australia on his own, but he had made the most significant contribution to the triumph by averaging 139.14 in the five matches. From an English point of view, something had to be done to constrain him, and that "something" escalated way beyond the confines of cricket.

Many millions of words have been written and spoken about the 1932/33 rubber, or the Bodyline series, as it became known. In essence, England had to find a way of halting Bradman's progress if they were to stand any chance of competing against Australia. Remove Bradman from the equation, or at least restrict his flow of runs, and they were evenly-matched sides.

▶ Douglas Jardine, England's captain in the Bodyline series, batting as usual in his Harlequins cap.

This sorry chapter in cricket's history has spawned endless theories about how the strategy of bowling short at the batsman's body came about. Some have involved the England captain, Douglas Jardine, sitting down to dinner with one of his predecessors, Arthur Carr, to hatch the plot. Carr was captain of Nottinghamshire, for whom Harold Larwood and Bill Voce were the fearsome fast bowlers who would execute the plan. Another theory was that the scheme was hatched on the ship bound for Australia. In all these scenarios Jardine was the central figure, and as such he was a much-hated figure in Australia. He did not help himself with a somewhat aloof manner and his habit of wearing his Oxford University Harlequins cap, widely regarded as a sign of disdain towards those of a lesser education and intellect. Add to that the charge of inventing Bodyline, and there was no reason to believe he could endear himself to the Australian public. But what that public did not realise was that Jardine himself was not responsible for the first application of leg theory, the less emotive term for the line of attack.

Jardine's vice-captain on that tour was Bob Wyatt, and in an interview given in 1990, the then 89-year-old Wyatt gave his account of how the strategy came about almost by accident. Wyatt believed that Jardine did entertain Carr at dinner while Nottinghamshire were playing at the Oval against Surrey in August 1932. It was a game in which Larwood took his 100th wicket of the season, and Voce also bowled well. Jardine would have known that this pair would form the spearhead of his attack in Australia, and so it was natural that he would have wanted to pick the brains of their county captain as to how to get the best out of them.

Wyatt also dismissed the idea that the strategy was formulated aboard ship, claiming instead that he had himself been the instigator. Shortly before the first Test, MCC (as England were known on tour outside Tests) played against an Australian XI in Melbourne. Jardine had taken the match off to go on a fishing expedition, leaving Wyatt in charge. It was a very fast wicket and the ball got old very quickly, so it ceased to swing away, and the Australians, including Bill Woodfull and Bradman, were having little difficulty in playing it on the on side. As the ball was not likely to leave the bat, Wyatt put one slip across, then another one and another with a view to stopping runs, not with the idea of intimidation. But Larwood was bowling very fast and batting was not pleasurable

when he occasionally dropped one short. Certainly Bradman was uncomfortable and even complained to the Australian Board of Control about the method of attack, which confirmed that England were on to something.

Larwood in that match was bowling with tremendous pace, and Wyatt remembered fielding at slip alongside Voce who said, "I hope to God they don't snick one, or it will go straight through us." Apparently the slips were ranged only some 30 yards away from the boundary, while wicket-keeper George Duckworth complained about the speed at which the ball was reaching him. Wyatt suggested he stood a little deeper, but Duckworth replied that he would not be able to reach the ball if he did because it was still rising when he took it above his head.

MCC were bowled out for just 60 in their second innings, the result of the fact that most of the party had been at a nightclub with the Nawab of Pataudi the previous evening. Wyatt realised that he was in line for criticism after such a poor showing and had a word with Larwood. "Now look, Harold," he said, "if Mr. Jardine comes back and we've been beaten, there'll be hell to pay." Larwood reassured him: "Don't worry skipper, I'll bowl them

◀ Bradman registers his first Ashes duck, dragging his first ball from Bill Bowes on to his stumps at the MCG.

out for you." In ideal conditions for him, with the wind directly behind and bowling down a slight slope, and the pitch greasy on top, he set about his task. Wyatt claims never to have seen speed like it but having taken two for five from 31 balls, Larwood was stopped by the rain and the match was drawn. One of those wickets was Woodfull and the other, Bradman, who was "frightened out and then bowled out".

After the match, when Jardine returned to the party, Wyatt told him what had happened. The captain commented, "That's very interesting; we'll pursue the matter." History records that he pursued it with such intensity that relations became strained, not only in cricketing circles but also right up to government level. Missives were exchanged in which fears were expressed for the friendly relations between two countries that had previously been the staunchest of Imperial allies.

There were no problems during the first Test at Sydney where Larwood took 10 wickets and Voce six, without employing leg theory. Stan McCabe scored a brilliant 187 not out, but could not prevent Australia from sliding to a 10-wicket defeat. It was during the second Test at Melbourne that Bodyline became apparent in Test cricket for the first time, and ironically, Australia won

that one by 111 runs on a pitch that had all the pace taken out of it to thwart the English attack. England had decided to play four fast bowlers and when conventional attack failed, Jardine heeded Wyatt's advice and ordered his fast men to bowl short at leg stump to a packed leg-side field.

It appeared that Australia had mastered the English as the press were claiming, reducing them to 30 for four in their first innings. It was not a promising position from which to press for a 338-run victory. Despite the defeat Larwood and Gubby Allen bowled magnificently on a good pitch, with Allen never employing a leg stump attack because, according to Wyatt, he was neither fast nor accurate enough to sustain it. But he did profit from the fact that when the batsmen had endured a dose of Larwood, they took liberties at the other end.

It was in the next Test at Adelaide, when Larwood felled Woodfull with a ball that hit him over the heart, that the balloon went up. Jardine, very foolishly in Wyatt's opinion, moved all the fielders onto the leg side to replicate the field set in the previous Melbourne encounter. The mood became even more volatile when Oldfield was hit on the head by a ball from Larwood, although the batsman later admitted that he should not have been trying to play such a quick

◀ The scoreboard at the SCG during the Bodyline Test of 1932.

delivery to leg from outside off stump.

Larwood blew Australia away again in Brisbane as England won by six wickets. Bradman did record a hundred runs – but spread over two innings as he fell to Larwood twice. In the final Test back in Sydney, England won by eight wickets as the diplomatic fall-out continued. Jardine escaped without censure by the authorities in England, however reviled he was in Australia, but Larwood became the scapegoat despite taking 33 Test wickets at 19.51 on that tour. He was never selected for his country again, and eventually retired, perfectly happily after some understandable initial apprehension, to live in Australia. Bradman averaged "only" 56.57 in the series, compared to his career average of 99.94.

With Larwood absent and Bradman in irresistible form, Australia regained the Ashes at the first attempt in 1934. Woodfull's team beat Wyatt's by 2-1, with two drawn in a fluctuating series. Australia won the first Test by 238 runs, with England taking the second by an innings and 38. The next two matches were high-scoring draws, setting up the Oval as the decider. Bradman's innings of 244 and another of 77, allied to 266 from Bill Ponsford, confirmed Australia as winners by a massive 562 runs. It was the start of a run of six series either side of the Second World War in which Australia were unbeaten.

By 1936-37, Bradman was at the helm in Australia, while Allen had assumed the captaincy of England. After convincing victories in the first two Tests, England appeared on course to regain the Ashes. But as Bradman and Hammond traded double hundreds, Australia fought back to win the remaining three matches by equally impressive margins.

Hammond captained England when Bradman brought his 1938 side on tour. Again, these two batting greats dominated as the first two Tests were drawn. Old Trafford was again the venue for the second of only three Ashes contests to be abandoned without a ball bowled, before Australia went one up at Headingley. At the Oval, Len Hutton, who had watched Bradman make his 334 at Headingley in 1930 as a 14-year-old, surpassed the Australian by compiling an innings of 364 in a quite superb display of batting and concentration. It was a timeless Test, and Hutton batted for exactly 800 minutes to set a new record for an individual innings in Test cricket. England won by an innings and 579 runs to square the series, but Australia retained their metaphorical grip on the urn. They did so before global hostilities once again belittled the importance of what was, after all was said and done, only a sport.

◄ The huge gas holders at the Oval dwarf the cricketers playing in front of them during the 1934 Test.

From Bradman To Benaud 1946–1961

As with the First World War, the Second resulted in an eight-year gap between Ashes contests. Of the missing members of the teams that had met at the Oval in 1938, the most poignant absence at the start of the 1946/47 series was that of Hedley Verity, the slow left arm Headingley-born bowler who had died of wounds as a prisoner of war in Italy three years earlier. "Keep going" were his last reported words to his platoon, after he was hit in the chest by gunfire during an attack on German positions in Sicily.

No doubt Verity would have wished Ashes contests to remain on track as well, and remarkably, four of England's 1938 batsmen took the field at the Gabba in Brisbane more than eight years later. Wally Hammond led them out, having

been persuaded to undertake one last tour at the age of 43. He was followed by the Middlesex "twins" Denis Compton and Bill Edrich as well as Len Hutton, who had himself been scarred by the conflict. An injury to his left arm during commando training had necessitated three bone grafts, and left the arm two inches shorter than his other.

The most notable Australian survivor, Don Bradman, was now 38, but after winning the toss he was not slow to reveal his continuing appetite and capacity for runs. Uncharacteristically shaky at the outset, The Don added 276 with Lindsay Hassett before being dismissed for 187, enabling Australia to reach 645. Successive thunderstorms then reduced the pitch to a classic Brisbane "sticky dog", upon which Keith Miller and Ernie Toshack made hay. Battle though they did, England had no answer, and Australia's win by an innings and 332 runs remains their most comprehensive in Ashes history, avenging England's innings and 579 run rout (still Test cricket's biggest) in that previous Ashes encounter of 1938.

Australia only needed to bat once in the next Test at Sydney, where Bradman and Sid Barnes both scored 234; their partnership of 405 remains a world Test record for the fifth wicket. The off spin of Ian Johnson and leg breaks of Colin McCool undid England this time, and it was all they could do to hold on for draws at Melbourne – where Australia ensured Ashes retention – and Adelaide. Baggy Green supremacy was underlined on a rain-affected pitch back at the SCG, where England were unfortunate to lose Hutton to tonsillitis after making a first innings hundred. Australia, with Ray Lindwall at his rapid best, prevailed by five wickets.

On his final tour to England in 1948, Bradman led "The Invincibles", one of the strongest Ashes teams ever fielded. In the first Test, he and Hassett again combined to help Australia pass 500 at Trent Bridge, where the job was completed by Miller and Bill Johnston. A record 132,000 people

attended the second Test at Lord's, but they could not help England, who were always playing catch-up after an Arthur Morris century launched the tourists. Lindwall – recovered from a groin injury – took seven wickets as Australia went two up, and Manchester rain again intervened to wash away England's Ashes hopes after 145 from Compton had helped them to a first innings lead. At Headingley, Australia emphasised their strength by scoring 404 to win on a turning wicket on day five, with Morris making 182 and Bradman an unbeaten 173.

As a seven-year-old spectator at the Oval for the final Test was not the only one with good reason to recall, that Headingley innings had produced the final run of a peerless career. England were shredded by Lindwall, dismissed for just 52 in their first innings at the Oval, and by the time Bradman, in what was known to be his last Test, was cheered to the wicket, the total was already 117 for one and the chances of Australia batting again were looking slim. By chance the wicket had fallen while the seven-year-old, impatient to watch Bradman bat, was buying an ice cream. So he heard the cheers from behind the stand, and before regaining his seat, the ensuing cheers as Bradman made his way back to the pavilion, bowled by the leg spinner Eric

◀ Don Bradman
walking out to
bat.

Hollies for a duck, second ball. Bradman had needed just four runs to end his Test career, and a significant era in cricket's history, with an average of 100. Morris made 196 to guide Australia to 389, and they duly won by an innings to take the rubber 4-0.

Any English hopes that Australia would be weaker for Bradman's retirement were swiftly snuffed out a little over two years later. England were certainly unfortunate with the weather at Brisbane, where Alec Bedser and Trevor Bailey, backed up by inspired wicket-keeping from Godfrey Evans, bowled the hosts out for 228. The ground was then hit by a thunderstorm that made the pitch venomous – a re-run of what had happened in 1946. Apart from a masterly, unbeaten 62 by Hutton, no batsman reached 20 in the remainder of the match, which England lost by 70 runs. The margin was tighter at Melbourne after Bailey and Bedser again gave England a good start, only to see the batsmen struggle against Lindwall, Miller, Johnston and the mystery spin of Jack Iverson, who was able to grip the ball between his thumb and a bent middle finger. He had learned this extraordinary technique while on army service in New Guinea, which has to rate as one of the more unlikely venues to affect

the outcome of the Ashes. Set 179 to win, England fell 28 runs short.

Iverson's finest hour came in the next Test at Sydney, where a wonderful all-round display by Miller gave Australia a substantial first innings lead. Needing 137 to make Australia bat again, England simply had no answer to Iverson's lively spin and bounce, losing by an innings and 13 runs as their Ashes hopes were once again ground to dust. Morris's highest Test score of 204 confirmed his team's superiority at Adelaide where only Hutton, who carried his bat for 156, resisted Australia for long. After a century on Test debut for Jim Burke, England were left needing 503 to win, and Miller, Johnson and Johnston ensured they fell well short. With the series gone, Bedser bowled England to a consolation win back at Sydney, something that was to occur remarkably often in the years that followed. It was Australia's first defeat in 26 Tests.

Bedser's path to bowling greatness scaled further heights in 1953. His 14 wickets at Trent Bridge gave Hutton's England a real chance of victory before the first Test was ruined by the weather, and he took eight more in a magnificent contest at Lord's, which ebbed and flowed as great Test matches should. It boiled down to a tense final day, sadly watched by just

◀ England captain Norman Yardley leads the cheers for Don Bradman in his final Test innings at the Oval.

▶ England
bowling great
Alec Bedser
demonstrates a
classic follow-
through on his
home ground at
the Oval.

14,000 people, which England, needing 343 to win, began at a parlous 20 for three. That became 73 for four when they lost Compton, but Bailey then joined Willie Watson to build one of the great defensive partnerships in Test history, let alone that of the Ashes. It was not so much the runs it added – 163 – but the time it took up to frustrate Australia's entirely justified victory hopes. Watson batted for five hours and 45 minutes before being dismissed for 109, while Bailey's 71 took four and a quarter hours. The ensuing draw that they had fought to secure was one of those that for England and their supporters felt more like a win.

Rain made its customary intervention at Old Trafford, but there was more last day excitement as Australia, needing a mere 43 runs to make England bat again, were almost bowled out short of that on a turning pitch. Bedser, Jim Laker and Johnny Wardle had reduced them to 35 for eight when time ran out. At Headingley though, despite another seven-wicket haul for Bedser, the bowling of Lindwall and Miller kept Australia on top. It was another never-say-die knock from Bailey – who occupied the crease for four hours and 20 minutes while making 38 – which saved England's bacon on the final day. It left

Australia needing 177 in just under two hours, and they finished 30 runs short. So to the decider at the Oval, and this time it was England who dominated, taking a

▼ Jack Iverson demonstrates his peculiar grip on a cricket ball.

▶ Leonard Hutton and Alec Bedser lead England out at the Oval in 1953, during the game in which they regained the Ashes after a 20 year absence.

small lead before Laker and Tony Lock span Australia out for 162. 132 needed, and although Australia made them work for it, England had lost just two wickets when Compton hit the winning runs to regain the Ashes for the first time since 1932/33.

It was a wonderful fillip for English cricket in Coronation Year, but Hutton's defence of the urn got off to a dreadful start at Brisbane in 1954/55. He put Australia in, they made 601 before declaring and England, with Evans incapacitated by sunstroke and Compton by a broken hand sustained on day one, subsided by an innings and 154 runs. At Sydney, however, they fought back and also unleashed a fast bowling sensation. Frank Tyson not only kept them in the game after they were put in and bowled out for 154; he then capitalised on a Peter May century by blowing Australia away. Well supported by Brian Statham, "The Typhoon" repeated the feat at the MCG after a glorious hundred from the young Colin Cowdrey to put England one up.

It was a remarkable comeback, and at Adelaide, England's freshly discovered new ball pairing (they could now afford to leave out Bedser) supported by Bailey and the lively off spin of Bob Appleyard, continued to flummox Australia. England were left

▼ Australia's record-breaking wicket-keeper Gilbert Langley.

needing just 94 to win the series and although Miller, never defeatist, had prized out Hutton, Edrich and Cowdrey with just 18 on the board, the tourists were guided safely to the target by Compton and Evans, ensuring both Ashes retention and a series win. The worst rain in New South Wales for half a century washed out the first three days back at the SCG, and despite forcing Australia to follow on England did not have time to secure a result.

Twelve hours of rain forced a similar outcome at Trent Bridge in the first match of the 1956 rubber, but at Lord's, Australia took advantage of Tyson's absence through injury to go one up. Miller, now 36 but still Australia's spearhead, took five wickets in each innings, while a vital knock of 97 from Richie Benaud ensured a telling lead for Australia. Remarkably the two wicket-keepers, Evans and Gilbert Langley, accounted for 16 of the wickets to fall, and Langley's nine dismissals (including Evans, stumped for a duck) established a Test record at the time. Again England had fallen behind, but again they were to come back, this time through a partnership not of pace but of spin, and the greatest individual bowling performance in Test history.

At Headingley, a sore knee prevented Miller from bowling and a partnership of 187 between May, now England's captain, and Cyril Washbrook rescued their team from the perils of 17 for three. Laker and Lock then worked their way through Australia, reducing them to 81 for six

before rain forced a delay of seven and a half hours. It also made life more difficult for the batsmen, and after following on, Australia succumbed to spin once again, Laker and Lock finishing with 18 wickets between them to level the series. At Old Trafford they took all 20, but rather less

evenly distributed.

Centuries from Peter Richardson and the Rev. David Sheppard helped England to 459, but were put into the shade by the events that followed. On a spin-friendly pitch that raised plenty of Australian eyebrows, Laker and Lock took 11 wickets

▲ Jim Laker is presented with the two balls with which he took 19 Australian wickets, still the world Test record, at Old Trafford in 1956.

on day two (Lock had just the one of them, with the first ball after tea) and Australia had followed on by the close. Rain then curtailed play to just two and a quarter hours on the Saturday and the Monday (Sunday was a rest day) and the wind was so strong on the Monday that heavy bails were deployed. But on the final day the weather relented, and as the sun dried the pitch, Laker span his way indelibly into history. Lock beat the bat regularly but unavailingly and it was Laker, with admirable close catching support, who wrought havoc. In one nine-over spell he dismissed Ian Craig, Ken Mackay, Miller and Ron Archer for just three runs, and with the ball spinning more sharply still after tea, he took the crucial wicket of Colin McDonald, who had resisted bravely for five and a half hours. When Len Maddocks fell lbw, England had retained the Ashes.

Laker's achievement was, and still is, without parallel. Finishing Australia with seven wickets for eight runs in 22 balls, he became the first bowler to take all 10 wickets in a Test innings (Anil Kumble was to emulate that feat for India against Pakistan 43 years later), but his record of 19 in the match, surpassing Sydney Barnes's 17 for England against South Africa in 1913, remains untouched. It is a mere footnote

◀ Jim Laker walks off the field at Old Trafford after taking all 10 Australian wickets for just 53 runs.

▶ The great Australian leg spinner Richie Benaud at the point of delivery at Old Trafford, scene of his great triumph in the 1961 Ashes Test. Fred Trueman is the watching batsman.

that this was the first Ashes result at Old Trafford since 1905, and the rain – such an influential factor there over the years – returned that very night to wash out first-class cricket throughout England the following day, and force a draw at the Oval to give England the series.

Against the expectations of most, Australia bounced back with a vengeance in 1958/59, thanks in large measure to Benaud's astute captaincy. Slow scoring by England at Brisbane – Bailey took 427 balls to make 68 – preceded a contrasting, unbeaten 78 by Norman O'Neill as Australia won just before a thunderstorm. Centuries from May and Neil Harvey followed at the MCG before Ian Meckiff and Alan Davidson set up a second Australian victory, dismissing the tourists for 87. After a hard-fought draw at Sydney, England were again outplayed at Adelaide, where McDonald scored 170 and Benaud took nine wickets with his leg spin to return the Ashes to Australia, before wrapping up the rubber 4-0 back in Melbourne.

Benaud was still in charge for Australia's next tour in 1961, and no less influential. England escaped with a draw at Edgbaston after being bowled out for 195 by Benaud and Mackay, but at Lord's, Australia went

one up on a lively pitch. A patient hundred from Bill Lawry followed a five-wicket haul from Davidson to put them ahead, and they were left needing just 69 to win, although Fred Trueman and Statham took five wickets before they got there. Trueman was to scale greater heights, again

in helpful conditions, on his home ground at Headingley in the next Test, taking 11 wickets to put England back on terms. The match of the series came at Old Trafford as Australia, after being behind almost throughout, snatched victory on the final day. With England needing 256, Benaud took the inspired decision to bowl round the wicket into the bowlers' footmarks. He took six wickets as England were reduced from 150 for one to 201 all out, and Australia had retained the Ashes. They made sure of the rubber in a high-scoring draw at the Oval.

The Urn In The
Balance 1962-1981

▶ Richie Benaud
taking advantage
of a Freddie
Trueman no ball
during the 1962
Brisbane Test.

When England headed Down Under for the 1962/63 series, attempting to bring back the urn that had been in Australian hands since the previous tour, they were led by Ted Dexter while Richie Benaud was still in charge of the home side. Dexter's instincts were all geared to playing attacking cricket, and in Benaud he had the perfect opponent to set up an audacious encounter. However, with the Ashes at stake there was little hope of reckless adventure from either side.

The first Test in Brisbane was a case in point. It was evenly matched throughout, but the Australians were comfortably in front towards the close of the fourth day. Rather than declaring then and having a go at England before stumps, Benaud closed the innings overnight, setting England 378 to win. The fact that they finished on 278 for six shows what might have been achieved by a less conservative declaration.

Benaud was in no position to set targets in Melbourne, where England won the second Test by seven wickets. They chased down 234 after Fred Trueman took five wickets to bowl out Australia before the close of the fourth day for 248. But England's euphoria at going 1-0 up was short-lived. Australia won the third Test on a turning Sydney pitch by eight wickets, bowling England out for a mere 104 in their second innings. An intriguing draw followed in Adelaide, while the final Test, back in Sydney, also ended in a draw after Dexter set Australia 241 to win, but not until well into the fifth day. Australia had made 152 for four when hands were

shaken to end a closely fought series that never quite caught fire. However cold they might have been, the Ashes remained with Australia.

Dexter had a final chance to break the Australian hold in 1964. Bobby Simpson had taken the reins of Australia from Benaud, who had retired, along with two other stalwarts, Neil Harvey and Alan Davidson, and there was considerable conjecture about the potential of the Australian side. Not for the first or last time, the perceived lack of quality brought out the best in the tourists, enough to retain the Ashes.

The first Test at Trent Bridge ended in a tense draw after rain washed out the third day. Two more lost days at Lord's prevented England from pressing home their advantage, and at Headingley, Australia needed only four days to win by seven wickets. England were bowled out for an unconvincing 268 in their first innings, but Australia appeared to be struggling themselves until Peter Burge took control. The burly Queenslander came in with his team prospering at 124 for two, but watched a clatter of wickets at the other end as his side declined to 178 for seven. He then found unlikely support from the tail until he was last out for a match-

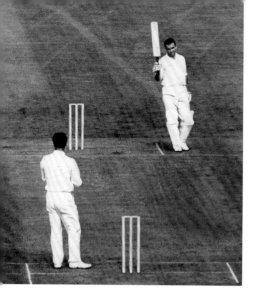

winning 160. After dismissing England for 229 Australia made 109 to win.

Simpson scored a triple hundred at Old Trafford to bat England out of that match and secure the Ashes once again, and at the Oval, England were always struggling to level the series once they were bowled out for 182. They did better second time around, but the match was drawn once again.

Simpson welcomed the bespectacled M.J.K. Smith to Australia in 1965/66. Smith, always known by his initials, led a side that based its strategy on attacking batting from the first ball. Bob Barber was renowned for this approach, but it was Geoff Boycott who surprised

many, including himself perhaps, by maintaining the form of his man-of-the-match performance in the previous season's domestic knock-out final at Lord's, where he won the Gillette Cup for Yorkshire against Surrey with a superb innings of 146.

Despite this positive approach, England's cause was not helped at Brisbane when a day was lost to rain. They were forced to follow on, and had only just passed Australia's first innings total with three wickets down at the close. They batted better at Melbourne, and more than held their own in a drawn match. In Sydney, Barber and Boycott helped England to victory by an innings and 93 runs. As on the previous expedition, Australia fought back immediately with an innings and nine-run victory in Adelaide, after Simpson and Bill Lawry put on 244 for the first wicket. So the series and the Ashes hinged on the fifth Test in Sydney. The fourth day was lost to the weather, but by then a triple hundred from Bob Cowper had put Australia in an unassailable position. The draw showed how evenly matched the sides were.

When Australia travelled to England in 1968, there was still broad parity between the sides captained by Lawry and Colin

◀ Bobby Simpson, who made 311 in the fourth Test at Old Trafford in 1964, acknowledges the applause of the Manchester crowd.

◀◀ Peter Burge was dismissed cheaply by Trueman in the first Test at Trent Bridge, but set up an Australian win in the third Test at Headingley.

Cowdrey, although once again the touring party was heralded as one of the weakest ever. It was still good enough to hold on to the Ashes for the fifth consecutive series since winning them so emphatically in 1958/59. They got off to a perfect start, winning at Old Trafford by 159 runs. Rain saved them at Lord's, where they were bowled out for 78 and forced to follow on 273 behind. They were 127 for four at the end of a match in which only about half the scheduled overs were bowled.

It was a similar story at Edgbaston, where the first day was lost to rain. England had the better of the draw, but looking back from a modern perspective it is difficult to have much sympathy given that their scoring rate was below two and a half runs an over throughout the series. Australia scored at just over two runs an over; Test cricket was not compelling viewing in this era. England again had the better of the draw at Headingley, before finally forcing a win to level the series at the Oval, where Derek Underwood took seven wickets in the fourth innings. There were only six minutes remaining when he took the final wicket, after a storm had flooded the ground at lunchtime. The ground staff were assisted by an army of volunteers from the crowd to make play possible.

That sagacious Yorkshireman then playing for Leicestershire, Ray Illingworth, led England to Australia in 1970/71, an expedition that regained the Ashes by a 2-0 margin. Illingworth was not liked by many Australians, and was regarded with suspicion even by some members of the English establishment, including the tour manager, D.G. Clark. He hailed from Kent and did not like the fact that Cowdrey was no more than vice-captain, a role to which he did not easily take. But the team as a whole gelled under Illingworth, and despite a succession of injuries overcame both the opposition and all other hurdles placed in his path. It was as a result of a complete washout at Melbourne on that tour, only the third in Ashes history, that one-day international cricket came into being.

England were on top in the Brisbane draw, while the Perth stalemate was more evenly balanced. After the washout, England won by 299 runs in Sydney, where John Snow bowled magnificently to take seven for 40 in the Australian second innings. The next attempt to play in Melbourne ended as a draw, as did the Adelaide Test, so the teams went to Sydney for the seventh match in the series with England still leading 1-0. An Australian win under their new captain, Ian Chappell,

◀ The entire England team appeal successfully for LBW against Australia's John Inverarity, to give Derek Underwood his seventh wicket and England victory at the Oval in 1968, squaring the series.

▶ A victorious
England team
carry their
captain Ray
Illingworth off
the field after
clinching the
Ashes in 1971.

would be enough to keep the Ashes in the Antipodes. When they dismissed England, without the injured Boycott and with Snow incapacitated during the match, for 184 in their first innings, the English management's decision to play the extra Test (for which they received no financial reward) appeared misconstrued. However, set 233 to win and with plenty of time available, Australia crumpled in their second innings for 160. The spirit that Illingworth had imbued in his men saw England to a historic triumph.

Compared with some of the stalemates that had been reached in the previous decade, the 1972 rubber was a classic, with Illingworth retaining England's hard-won Ashes. They went one up at Old Trafford, but an unheralded swing bowler by the name of Bob Massie wrote himself into the record books with an astonishing eight wickets in each innings as Australia levelled at Lord's. After a draw at Trent Bridge, England secured the urn on a disease-affected pitch at Headingley, where Underwood and Illingworth spun their side to a nine-wicket win. So to the Oval, where a stand of 201 for the third wicket between the Chappell brothers, Ian and Greg, steered Australia towards equality in the rubber and set the tone for what was to

follow in the next two series.

That of 1974/75 was dominated by as fearsome – and good – a pair of fast bowlers to have appeared in Ashes encounters. Dennis Lillee had suffered a bad back injury in the West Indies in 1973, but came back magnificently to hunt down England's batsmen with Jeff Thomson, who had made an inconspicuous debut against Pakistan two years earlier. While Lillee had a classical action and every skill at the fast bowler's disposal, Thomson relied on a slinging action and sheer speed to wreak his part of the havoc that ensued. They were backed by an outstanding team of all the talents, led by the uncompromising Ian Chappell.

Australia won the first Test by 166 runs and the second in Perth by nine wickets, where the 41-year-old Colin Cowdrey was plucked from a dank English winter to face Thomson and Lillee on one of the fastest pitches in the world. It was just four days after his arrival in Australia, with England's batting line-up decimated by injury. Cowdrey went in first wicket down in the first innings and opened in the second, when he batted as well as anybody. After arriving at the crease for the first time, he found himself wandering towards the drinks trolley with "Terror" Thomson. He

▶ Australian swing bowler Bob Massie is applauded off by his team-mates after taking a phenomenal 16 wickets on his Ashes debut, at Lord's in 1972.

introduced himself with the words: "I don't believe we've met. My name's Cowdrey."

The Boxing Day Test at Melbourne was drawn, but it was anything but drab. The first three innings produced a top score of 244, by England in their second innings, leaving Australia 246 to win. They reached the mandatory last hour of 15 overs needing another 55 with four wickets in hand. With the spinners operating, seven runs were added in the first seven of those overs. It appeared that Australia were playing for the draw, so England captain Mike Denness took the new ball, only for Rod Marsh to mount an assault upon it. After 13 overs, 16 were needed with three wickets in hand, but the batsmen took no risks after another wicket fell. The match ended with Australia eight wickets down and eight runs short of victory.

Australia won easily in Sydney, where Denness dropped himself due to poor form, and equally easily in Adelaide, with Denness restored but Thomson injured while playing tennis on the rest day. He was absent from the sixth Test as England enjoyed themselves, winning by an innings and four runs after Denness and Keith Fletcher – two of the batsmen to suffer most against the Lillee/Thomson combination – both scored big hundreds in

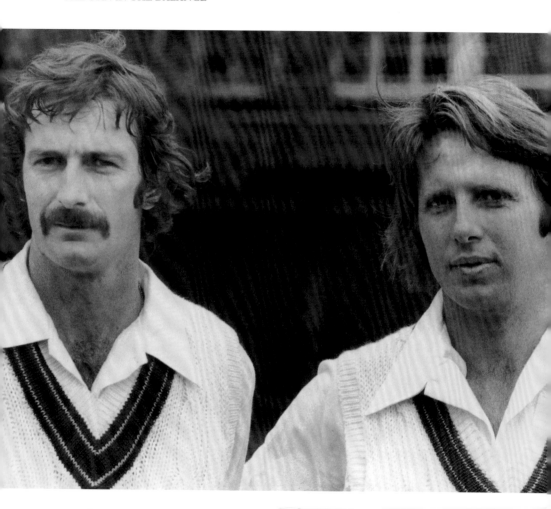

a fourth wicket partnership worth 192.

Tony Greig replaced Denness after one match of the 1975 series, which was confined to a mere four encounters after the World Cup. At Edgbaston, Denness had gambled on the weather and sent Australia in to bat. The gamble failed and Denness lost his job. He was replaced in the side for Lord's by David Steele, a grey-haired, bespectacled batsman plucked from the obscurity of county cricket with Northamptonshire, but Steele became a national hero with a show of defiance against the might of Lillee and Thomson. A draw at headquarters was followed by two more at Leeds (where the pitch was vandalised) and the Oval. Had the Australian hold on the Ashes been loosened?

The answer was that it had, but not only by English resistance. There was additional help, ironically from an Australian. The name of Kerry Packer was not to be found in any batting or bowling averages, but the disruptive influence of the television mogul, who was in the process of buying up most of the Australian team, and some key figures in England's, loomed large across the 1977 series. Tony Greig was Packer's chief recruiting officer in England, and by taking the Packer shilling he lost the captaincy. Mike Brearley replaced him, and

if he was only a marginal Test player, he was an outstanding leader. The Australians hated him for it.

The series began at Lord's with a weather-affected draw from which Australia retreated with the greatest relief. There was no such escape at Old Trafford, where England won by nine wickets. The margin at Trent Bridge was seven wickets, despite Boycott running out local hero Derek Randall on his way to a hundred. A certain I.T. Botham marked his Test debut with five wickets in Australia's first innings. Boycott's hundred at Headingley, on his home ground, was his 100th in first-class cricket and helped England to win by an innings and 85 runs. The Oval Test was drawn as Greg Chappell's Australians left England, and Test cricket, for some time.

When competition resumed in 1978/79 in Australia, Brearley's England were vastly superior to Graham Yallop's Packer-weakened Australians. Despite a heroic effort by Rodney Hogg, who took a record 41 wickets in the six-match series, England reeled off five wins out of six. It was an emphatic, if slightly hollow triumph. It was also reversed just a year later, when England returned to Australia for a double tour with the West Indies as the Australian stars returned to the fold. Australia won 3-0, but

◀ Australia's lethal fast bowling partnership of the 1970s, Dennis Lillee and Jeff Thomson.

► Ian Botham batting at Old Trafford, 1981.

the Ashes were not at stake.

They were back on the agenda in 1981, when it looked for the entire world as if they would be returning to Australia after two matches. They won a low scoring encounter at Trent Bridge by four wickets, but were on the wrong end of a draw at Lord's. Meanwhile Botham had been finding the England captaincy a wearisome burden, which was affecting his form as a batsman and bowler. He bagged a pair at Lord's, and as he walked back to the pavilion after his second, fruitless innings, the eerie silence that accompanied him every step of the way spelt the end of his reign. Brearley was brought back, with spectacular results.

At Headingley, England on day four were as good as beaten. Bookmakers were offering odds of 500-1 against an England victory that tempted those arch Australians Mssrs. Lillee and Marsh to invest a small part of their expected win bonus on the most unlikely result. After following on, England were still 92 behind as the seventh second innings wicket fell, but Botham was sensational. With Graham Dilley offering support way beyond his usual batting means, Botham smashed his way to 149 not out and England set Australia a paltry

130 to win. Bob Willis then enjoyed his finest hour as he took eight for 43 to power England to an 18-run victory, superbly controlled by Brearley.

It was Botham the bowler who brought England back from the brink at Edgbaston in the next Test. Australia, needing 151 to win, had reached 114 for five. Botham had been left to ruminate in the field by Brearley, who now chose exactly the right moment to unleash him. The result? England won by 29 runs after Botham returned figures of 14-9-11-5, with those five wickets coming in the space of 28 balls for the cost of one run. Lightning had struck twice in two matches. It could not strike again in Manchester, could it?

Yes it could, or Botham could. England had a first innings lead of 101, but batting again had only extended that by 104 at the fall of the fifth wicket, when Botham strode to the crease. By the time he left, just a couple of hours later with 118 to his name, the lead was 354. With the lower order taking toll of a demoralised attack, Australia were set a target of 506 to win and fell short by 103. The Ashes were safe again, leaving England to hang on for a draw at the Oval, but it could have all been so different had it not been for Botham and Brearley.

▶ Jubilant English fans celebrate after the historic victory at Edgbaston in 1981.

From Botham To
Warne 1982-2007

The 1982/83 series fulfilled an
ambition for Greg Chappell, once
again Australia's captain, to regain the
Ashes held by England since 1977. Ian
Botham was not as fit as he had been a
year earlier, and England, with several
leading players banned for taking part in
an unofficial tour of South Africa, were
below full strength. A draw at Perth was
marred by an injury to Terry Alderman,
who dislocated his shoulder rugby-tackling
a spectator during a pitch invasion. But in
his absence Geoff Lawson, Jeff Thomson
and Rodney Hogg helped Australia to
successive wins in Brisbane and Adelaide.

The Melbourne Test was one of the
all-time Ashes thrillers, with Australia,
apparently destined for a four-day defeat
on 218 for nine chasing 292, taking the

match into the last day thanks to the last-
wicket pair of Allan Border and Thomson.
Needing another 37 on the final morning,
they eked out runs to such effect that when
Botham began the 18th over of the day,
they needed just four to win. Thomson
immediately edged a short ball to second
slip, where an anxious Chris Tavare could
merely parry it. Tragically for Australia and
mercifully for England, it rebounded up
rather than down for Geoff Miller to run
round from first slip to catch it. The series
had new life, but Australia had the better
of a Sydney draw to wrench the urn from
England's grasp.

Botham's all-round influence – and a
dogged 175 from Tim Robinson – helped
England go one up at Headingley in 1985,
but at Lord's one of Border's Olympian

efforts – 196 – combined with the bowling of Lawson and Craig McDermott to pull Australia back. After high-scoring draws at Trent Bridge and Old Trafford, the balance shifted decisively at Edgbaston, thanks to the selection of Richard Ellison, who took 10 wickets, and the batting of David Gower, now England's captain, whose 215 was to remain his best Test score.

The eventual result at Edgbaston was influenced by a freak dismissal on the final afternoon. With Australia battling to avoid defeat, their wicket-keeper, Wayne Phillips, who had resisted stubbornly for 59, hit a

ball from Phil Edmonds hard into the instep of Allan Lamb, taking evasive action at silly point. The ball ballooned up for Gower to catch it, and after the bowler's umpire David Shepherd consulted David Constant at square leg, the unfortunate Phillips was given out. There was little further resistance as England won by an innings, and Ellison's swing bowling matched up with a wonderful stand of 351 between Graham Gooch and Gower at the Oval to ensure yet another change of Ashes tenure.

One of Botham's finest Test innings (138) saw England off to a surprise win at Brisbane in the 1986/87 opener after Mike Gatting's England had struggled in all departments in the build-up. High-scoring draws followed at Perth and Adelaide, but at the MCG, England were emphatically the better side. Botham and Gladstone Small picked Australia off before Chris Broad, who enjoyed an excellent series, scored a hundred to give the tourists a healthy lead. They did not need to bat again, and although a big hundred from Dean Jones set up an Australian win in Sydney, the urn remained in English hands.

The fact that they have not defended it successfully since is indicative of Australia's strength and England's decline to the point where, in the mid-1990s,

they were labelled the worst team in the world. Australia's revival owed much to the nuggety captaincy of Border, a man driven by experience of the years of failure. He was at the crease at Headingley when Australia won the first Test of the 1989 series, propelled by the recovered Alderman (10 wickets) and the emerging Steve Waugh, whom Gower's England simply could not dislodge. Waugh's 177 at Leeds preceded 152 at Lord's, where Australia again passed 500 and Alderman struck nine more times, putting them two up.

But for rain at Edgbaston they would probably have won there as well, although Gus Fraser did manage to dismiss Waugh for the first time (his series average now stood at 393). It was only the second time an English pace bowler had hit the stumps in the series. Waugh was again Australia's top scorer at Old Trafford, and along with Alderman and Lawson forced England to surrender the Ashes with two games remaining, despite a battling, unbeaten century from wicket-keeper Jack Russell that gave Australia a small target to chase. There was no such requirement at Trent Bridge, where England were annihilated from day one, as openers Geoff Marsh and Mark Taylor posted 301 without being parted. Australia controlled the drawn finale

◀ Paul Downton and Mike Gatting celebrate the dismissal of Wayne Phillips in the 1985 Ashes series.

at the Oval, and Border had become their first captain since Woodfull in 1934 to regain the Ashes in England.

Their grip on the urn was to remain firm for 16 years, as the team went from strength to strength. In the 1990/91 series England again failed to win a Test, and were further tormented by Alderman as Australia took just three days to secure a 10-wicket win in Brisbane. The lanky left arm pace bowler Bruce Reid was their destroyer at the MCG, with 13 wickets before Marsh and David Boon saw Australia comfortably to a target of 197. Draws followed at Sydney and Adelaide, the latter featuring a century on debut for Steve Waugh's twin brother Mark. At Perth, Alderman, McDermott and Merv Hughes were rampant as Australia made it 3-0.

The chasm between the two teams hereabouts was about as great as any in Ashes history. In 1993, England did manage their first win in three rubbers, but only after being beaten four times. The first Test at Old Trafford will always be remembered for the "ball of the century", Shane Warne's first in Ashes cricket, which span in apparent defiance of the laws of geometry to hit Gatting's off stump after pitching well outside leg. Warne took eight wickets as Australia went one up, and eight more at Lord's as England were trounced. Taylor, Boon and Michael Slater all made hundreds as Australia posted 632. They did not need to bat again.

England competed at Trent Bridge, with hundreds for the two Grahams, Gooch and Thorpe, but could not force victory, and were routed again at Headingley, where a Border double century saw Australia to the heights of 653 for four declared. The bats of Mark Waugh and wicket-keeper Ian Healy and the spin of Warne and Tim May compounded England's misery at Edgbaston, and their win at the Oval roused the inevitable suspicion that the rampant Australians had taken their collective foot off the pedal.

It was a triumphant Ashes farewell for Border, while Gooch resigned the England captaincy after the Headingley defeat, making way for Mike Atherton. Border himself was succeeded by Taylor, who quickly proved a worthy successor in 1994/95. Big hundreds from Slater and Mark Waugh got his reign off to a winning start at the Gabba, where McDermott and Warne shared 19 wickets, and they took another 17 as Australia went two up at the MCG. At Sydney, Darren Gough gave England hope, with six scalps as Australia were bundled out for 116, but a big stand

◀ Steve Waugh on his way to 177 not out during the first Test at Headingley, 1989.

◀◀ Ian Botham at the crease during his innings of 138 at the first Test in Brisbane, 1986.

between Taylor and Slater kept the tourists at bay. With Ashes hopes extinguished England revived at Adelaide, with Devon Malcolm and Chris Lewis ensuring victory after Gatting scored what was to be his last Test century. But at Perth normal service was resumed; a certain Glenn McGrath got amongst England's top order on the fourth day, and Australia wrapped up the series 3-1. He was to account for one of his victims, Atherton, a world record 19 times.

McGrath's three Perth wickets were but an hors d'oeuvre for the tasty fare he was to serve up for Australia over more than a decade, as he and Warne equated the value of three bowlers, allowing them the luxury of needing to play only four. Their 1997 confidence was jolted, however, in the first Test at Edgbaston, where Gough and Andrew Caddick skittled them for 118. A memorable partnership of 288 between Nasser Hussain (207) and Thorpe (138) gave England a healthy lead, and although hundreds for Taylor and Greg Blewett took Australia to 477, England chased down the target comfortably. At Lord's though, they were probably saved by rain as McGrath showed immediate mastery of the conditions and famous slope, with eight for 38 as England were dismissed for 77.

Back-to-back centuries from Steve Waugh boosted Australia further at Old Trafford, where McGrath and Warne finished the job, while at Headingley, England were dismantled first by Jason Gillespie and then by Paul Reiffel. In between, Matthew Elliott was dropped three times on his way to 199, and Ricky Ponting made his maiden Test century on his Ashes debut. At Nottingham, Australia

retained the Ashes once more, with their third win on the trot built on depth of batting and with McGrath and Warne again to the fore. Although Caddick and Phil Tufnell consigned Australia to another Oval defeat, their 3-2 victory margin flattered England.

Retaining the Ashes with a game or two in hand was now an Australian habit, evident again in 1998/99. Although Alec Stewart's England escaped with a draw at Brisbane, they fell foul of Gillespie and Damien Fleming in Perth. At Adelaide, Justin Langer made 179, the first of five Ashes tons, before McGrath, Fleming and Stuart MacGill, replacing the injured Warne, got amongst England and once more the fate of the urn was prematurely decided. Again England won belatedly, in a fine match at Melbourne as Australia, needing just 175 to win, fell 13 runs short as the Kent pace bowler Dean Headley enjoyed his finest hour. But the rubber nonetheless ended 3-1 after a 12-wicket haul for MacGill clinched the Test at Sydney, despite a hat-trick for Gough.

The destiny of the Ashes could hardly have been settled more quickly than it was in 2001. Australia's four-man attack of McGrath, Gillespie, Warne and Brett Lee was much too strong for England

▶ Glenn McGrath celebrates taking the wicket of Devon Malcolm during the fifth Test at Trent Bridge, 1997.

at Edgbaston, where wicket-keeper Adam Gilchrist followed centuries from Steve Waugh, now leading Australia, and Damien Martyn with a sensational 152, at better than a run a ball. Hussain's captaincy dilemmas were emphasised by his decision to call upon the gentle pace of Mark Butcher, who remarkably took four

wickets. McGrath again excelled at Lord's, and although England did manage to set Australia a target, it was only 14.

Warne tormented England further at Trent Bridge as Australia took just three days to ensure Ashes retention, and a series win. This time England's consolation came at Headingley, where Butcher played the

▲ Justin Langer batting during the third Test at Adelaide in 1998.

innings of his life, an unbeaten 173, to make the most of a sporting declaration. At the Oval, Steve Waugh, less than 100% fit and virtually batting on one leg, was one of three centuries as Australia again passed 600 and completed England's humiliation.

Hussain surely contributed to England's woeful start in the 2002/03 series by putting Australia in at Brisbane, only to see Matthew Hayden (197) and Ponting (123) help them to 492. Eventually set 464 to win, England folded to Warne and McGrath for a paltry 79. Amid another innings defeat at Adelaide, England drew some comfort from a high-class innings of 177 from Michael Vaughan. At the WACA, Australia again needed to bat just once to retain the Ashes, and at Adelaide, Langer made 250 out of their 551. Even another sublime innings of 145 from Vaughan could not save England after they followed on, but his knock of 183 at the SCG confirmed his status as the world's premier batsman before Caddick bowled England to victory.

Successive 4–1 score lines would not have led Australia, now captained by Ponting, to return to English shores with anything other than sure confidence in 2005. And when McGrath yet again bowled England over – including his 500th

Test wicket – in his valedictory appearance at Lord's, it seemed that their winning streak against other teams under Vaughan was about to be put starkly into context. But as cricket lovers the length and breadth of the country sighed with despair, how could they have known that they were about to witness what was likely to be the series of a lifetime?

Much as Hussain had erred three years earlier, Ponting helped to initiate a shift in the balance by putting England in at Edgbaston. Marcus Trescothick, Kevin Pietersen and Andrew Flintoff responded so positively that England passed 400, but although they took a solid lead, their dismissal by Warne and Lee for 182 left Australia needing 282 to go two up. At 137 for seven they seemed out of it, but an aggressive 42 from Warne was followed by a last-wicket partnership between Lee and Michael Kasprowicz which, just like that between Border and Thomson at the MCG 23 years earlier, edged Australia inexorably closer. They were just three runs short when a ball from Stephen Harmison brushed Kasprowicz's glove on its way through to wicket-keeper Geraint Jones.

England's winning margin of two runs – one less than that Melbourne classic – remains the smallest in Ashes history, but it

enabled them to head for Old Trafford with renewed spirit, knowing that their four-man pace attack of Harmison, Matthew Hoggard, Flintoff and Simon Jones posed a real threat. So it proved in another great Test match, which England came within a wicket of winning at the last gasp. Two captains' innings, from Vaughan on day

▲ Glenn McGrath with his gold "500 wicket" boots.

◄ A jubilant Matthew Hayden and Ricky Ponting after Australia retained the Ashes at Perth in 2002.

► The England team celebrate after winning the final fifth Ashes Test match against Australia, 2005.

one and Ponting on day five, Warne's 600th Test wicket, and the pace of Jones, who constantly harried Australia, were among the memorable features, and Australian celebrations at having escaped defeat did not go unnoticed by England's captain.

By the end of the next encounter at Trent Bridge cricket's profile in England had rocketed, along with the heart rates of those who could scarcely bear to watch for the tension. An eye-catching Flintoff hundred helped England to 477, before

combination of Hoggard and Ashley Giles cool headedly saw them past the post. So a win or a draw would be enough at the Oval, but with England at 127 for five at lunch on the final day, just 133 ahead, Australia were fancying their chances. That was when Pietersen came of age as a Test cricketer with a scintillating 158, ensuring the draw that returned the Ashes to England for the first time since 1987.

Amid the national rejoicing, honours were awarded to every member of the

Hoggard and Jones forced Australia to follow on. Although England were left needing just 129, the wiles of Warne and pace of Lee, to say nothing of the mind-scrambling tension, had them tottering at 116 for seven before the unlikely

◀ Kevin Pietersen, who played such a crucial role for England on the final day of the 2005 Ashes series.

England team, but it was Australia who learned from their defeat. In 2006/07 they took comprehensive revenge, thrashing England 5-0. From the moment Harmison sent the first ball of the series straight to second slip, the tone was set. It was maintained by 196 from Ponting, and Australia won by an innings after passing 600. The nadir was reached at Adelaide where England contrived to lose after declaring on 551 for six, following a stand of 310 between Paul Collingwood (206) and Pietersen (158). Warne was instrumental in dismissing England cheaply after Australia had passed 500 in reply, and they won by six wickets.

England's resolve was certain to be dented by such a reversal, and the margins of defeat that followed – 206 runs at Perth to end their Ashes tenure of little more than a year, an innings and 99 runs inside three days at Melbourne, and 10 wickets in Sydney – tell clearly of the most one-sided Ashes contest since 1920/21. England undoubtedly missed Vaughan's captaincy (Flintoff deputised), as well as Trescothick and Simon Jones, while the question for Australia, who faced the next encounter without Warne, McGrath, Gilchrist and Langer, was whether they could find replacements approaching such calibre.

◀ The Australian team celebrate regaining the Ashes with a 5-0 whitewash, January 2007.

The Ashes Rekindled
2009

The dawn of a new Ashes year in 2009 was hardly a glad, confident morning for either of the two protagonists. Australia, shorn of key players since their 2006/07 whitewash, entered the year with their position at the head of the World Test Championship under serious threat. After losing the Test series in India 2-0, they lost a home series for the first time in 16 years to South Africa, the team widely regarded as the likely inheritors of Australia's crown. Meanwhile, England's confidence could hardly have been boosted after they too were beaten in India, by the peremptory departures of both their captain and their coach.

It should be noted that England's defeat in India was surrounded by exceptional circumstances. While being soundly beaten in the one-day series preceding the Tests, England hastily departed the country in the aftermath of the Mumbai atrocities. The players were lauded for returning to India for the hurriedly rearranged Test series, and surprised possibly even themselves by dominating the first three and a half days of the initial encounter in Chennai. India's batsmen eventually wrested victory from them before defending the lead at Mohali. To have won in India, or even drawn, would have whipped up unhealthy expectations in comparison with Australia's performance, yet the different circumstances rendered any such comparisons worthless. While much was made of England's state of mind on their return to India, little was made of how the home players might have been feeling after the Mumbai tragedy, and

▶ How many of these Australians will participate in the 2009 Ashes series?

the English performance should be viewed in this context.

It is always a boon for a player to be able to retire of his own volition in triumphant circumstances. For Justin Langer, Glenn McGrath and Shane Warne, the end of the Sydney Ashes Test in 2007 provided the optimum moment. Of these three, Warne was quite simply irreplaceable. His long-term understudy, Stuart MacGill, has since retired as well, and the selectors' problem has been illustrated by their tendency to use bit-part spinners, Andrew Symonds, Michael Clarke and Cameron White amongst them. But it has also to be remembered that English batsmen have a sorry history of being vulnerable to any spin bowler, not necessarily of the highest class.

McGrath cannot be replaced in terms of experience, but amongst his successors the left arm paceman Mitchell Johnson has been described by the legendary Dennis Lillee as the "bowler of a decade". Peter Siddle has shown promise, but Stuart Clark has a worrying elbow injury that makes his full potential (considerable in English conditions) doubtful. Brett Lee missed the tour of South Africa because of ankle surgery after struggling for form at home, and Symonds has also had an

◀ England all-rounder Andrew Flintoff, potentially a pivotal figure in the 2009 series, working on his fitness.

◀◀ England captain Andrew Strauss (right) and wicket-keeper Matt Prior.

LITTLE BOOK OF THE ASHES 105

Stuart Broad is a steadily improving bowler for England who has also shown potential with the bat.

operation on his knee.

Other great Australian names have departed since 2007. Adam Gilchrist's successor, Brad Haddin, is a tidy wicket-keeper and competent batsman, but nowhere near as explosive as Gilchrist and will not strike fear in the opposition's hearts to the same degree. And Matthew Hayden's dreams of emulating Langer's triumphant exit crumbled to dust as injury and loss of form persuaded him that the end of the series against South Africa was the time to bow out. Much depends on the continuing consistency of Ricky Ponting, as well as the now established Mike Hussey, no stranger to English conditions, and vice-captain Clark.

England's plans to go into the Ashes series with Peter Moores and Kevin Pietersen as respective coach and captain were torn apart when the rift between the two became public knowledge early in the year. The appointment of Andrew Strauss as captain was a formality, not least given his successful, if brief, tenure in place of the injured Michael Vaughan in 2006. Vaughan, so inspirational in England in 2005 and so missed in 2006/07, could yet return to the batting ranks, while Pietersen, a still better batsman now than he was then, remains key to English hopes. Gone

though, are Marcus Trescothick, due to a stress-related illness, and Ashley Giles, with a recurring hip ailment.

In the pace department Andrew Flintoff is back almost to his best as a bowler, albeit one whose fitness is destined to be fragile, but question marks hang over the other three who played in 2005. Matthew Hoggard seems to have gone for good, but James Anderson or a fit Ryan Sidebottom could be just as effective. Simon Jones remains injury prone, but Stuart Broad is emerging as an adequate replacement and potential all-rounder, while Stephen Harmison continues to blow hot and cold. As to spin, the value of Giles is more apparent now he has gone; Monty Panesar is thought to be a better bowler (albeit inferior batsman and fielder) but has not really progressed, while Graeme Swann and Adil Rashid are seen as possible replacements. The wicket-keeping slot, handed back to Matt Prior at the turn of the year, is no more settled than it has been for some years.

So England, with the position of head coach unfilled and persistent rumours of dressing room rifts, began back-to-back series against the West Indies in the Caribbean knowing that only consecutive victories would enable them

to go into the Ashes with confidence. Australia, meanwhile, had the tricky task of attempting to avenge their home defeat on South African turf, with Ponting's captaincy under increasing scrutiny. Both camps still had the scope to tweak their existing teams ahead of the Ashes series.

With so many of the quality players involved in the legendary 2005 rubber now departed or doubtful starters, it would be wildly optimistic to expect this latest encounter to match it in quality, intensity or excitement. So perhaps the anticipation that attended the build-up to that contest, then widely considered to be between the two best teams in the world, should be tempered with rather more caution. Despite Australia's many changes in personnel, they should start as narrow favourites.

But such is cricket's glorious unpredictability, and so volatile does the World Test Championship Table now look, that the ancient contents of that famous little urn could blaze fiercely once more. If so, in an uncertain, helter-skelter era so pervaded by Twenty20 and the fast dollar, they could brightly illuminate Test cricket as the inimitably best form of the grand old game in which leather meets willow.

Andy Flower, who was appointed England Team Director in April 2009.

Venues For The Ashes 2009

First Test – Cardiff, 8th-12th July

The recently redeveloped SWALEC Stadium in Cardiff, which will be the venue for the first 2009 Ashes Test.

There was criticism of the England and Wales Cricket Board when Lord's was announced as the venue for the first Ashes Test of 2005. England duly lost the opener and the cries became even louder that the series should have begun somewhere like Edgbaston, a ground renowned for its noisy, even rowdy patriotism as opposed to the more sedate and polite Lord's. Imagine then, the howls of outrage when the venue for the first Ashes Test of 2009 was announced as Cardiff.

The governing body of English cricket might be known as the England and Wales Cricket Board, but the Welsh presence disappears in the abbreviation ECB. Although Glamorgan play in the English County Championship, there is a greater history of sporting rivalry between the Welsh and English than there is of co-operation. Ask anyone who has put on a white shirt and played rugby in the Millennium Stadium, or even the old Arms Park. The authorities hope that the transformation of the cricket ground from Sophia Gardens to the SWALEC Stadium will conquer a phobia of things English in Wales, and that there will be capacity crowds every day of the Test in July, cheering itself hoarse for England.

The reason for the choice of Cardiff ahead of the traditional venues of Old Trafford or Trent Bridge has nothing to do with cricket. It is entirely finance-driven. The Welsh Assembly underwrote

a guarantee to the ECB that meant the economic argument could not be bettered, as well as pledging £10 million to bring

the ground up to Test standard. The square was turned around through 90 degrees, a new pavilion, media centre

and stands were constructed, but nothing could be done about the River Taff, which curtailed development along one side of the ground, a well-timed chip away from the middle. Not only does that impose cricketing restrictions, with captains reluctant to expose certain bowlers to a close and watery leg-side boundary, but even with extra seating brought in for the Ashes the capacity will be no more than 19,000. On the final day at Old Trafford in 2005 there were 10,000 people locked out and 23,000 inside.

Old Trafford also boasts one of the best cricket wickets in the country, where England have been successful in five of the six previous Tests played there. The sixth? The unforgettable Ashes draw of 2005. Trent Bridge also has conditions conducive to good cricket and like Old Trafford, a history of successfully staging Test matches. Cardiff has staged one-day internationals since 1999, when Australia were beaten by New Zealand in the group stages of the World Cup. Australia beat Pakistan there in 2001, and also played on the ground, in its old format, in 2005 when they were spectacularly beaten by Bangladesh. Are these bad memories the reason behind the decision to award Cardiff its first Test? Probably not, because England have played

◀ The headquarters of English cricket, Lord's, will stage the second Ashes Test in 2009.

two one-day internationals on the ground and both were washed out.

However the venue is viewed, there is no doubt that the authorities are taking a massive risk by staging this first Test in Cardiff. The infrastructure and the pitch are untested for such a large event, and deficiencies in either will result in a severe loss of face, and confidence in the ECB. The stakes are high, possibly too high for such a gamble to be justified.

Second Test – Lord's, 16th-20th July

England have played against Australia 34 times in Tests at Lord's. 14 have ended as draws, while of the remaining 20, dating back to 1884, England have won five to Australia's 15. This is not a good ground for England. The last time they beat Australia in London NW8 was in 1934, when Hammond and Sutcliffe strode across the famous turf to take England to an innings and 38-run success. The Australians did not have a bad side at the time, with the likes of Bradman, Grimmett and O'Reilly in the team. It was England's only win in the series.

Since then, nine of the 18 matches have been draws and Australia have won the

other nine, as the opposition have tended to be inspired by the atmosphere of cricket's headquarters rather than the home side. It does not augur well for England, and there is no comfort in looking back in history to find the only other Anglo-Australian Test to begin on July 16th. That was in 1888, and despite the presence of W.G. Grace, England failed by 61 runs to reach their target of 124.

Third Test – Edgbaston, July 30th-August 3rd

Test matches between England and Australia were not staged in Birmingham until 1902, since when there have been 11 more encounters. The balance at Edgbaston is with England, who have won five matches to Australia's three, with four draws. The England players enjoy playing on this ground, because of the support they receive. No other Test venue in England can guarantee such patriotic fervour, generated notably from the Eric Hollies Stand as it is now named, after the England and Warwickshire leg-spinner who bowled Bradman for nought in his last Test appearance at the Oval in 1948. The noise gets noticeably louder as the day wears on and the beer starts to talk.

◀ Play under way at Warwickshire CCC's Edgbaston ground, despite threatening clouds overhead. The third Ashes Test of 2009 will be played here.

Three of England's wins at Edgbaston have been big ones, by 10 wickets in 1909, an innings and 118 runs in 1985 and nine wickets in 1997. All three of Australia's victories on this ground have been by similar margins, an innings and 85 runs in 1975, eight wickets in 1993 and an innings and 118 runs in 2001. England's famous win in 1981 was by only 29 runs, but even that does not compare with 2005 when the margin was a mere two runs after one of the most thrilling matches imaginable. Chasing 282 to win, Australia began the fourth day on 175 for eight, and the question on everybody's lips was whether it would be all over in two balls or two overs. It took 21 overs of gradually increasing tension before what could easily have been the winning stroke led to the winning catch. Edgbaston is a result ground if the weather holds.

Fourth Test – Headingley, 7th–11th August

With 25 days of Test cricket scheduled to be played in 40 days, fitness and stamina, both mental and physical, will play a crucial role in the 2009 series. By the time the players reach Leeds, injuries will almost certainly have played a part and the fitness

of the bowlers will be most important. If the Yorkshire sky is overcast, the ball is likely to swing round corners if the bowlers possess the skills to make it do so, but should the sun shine, batsmen will enjoy themselves. 23 Ashes Tests have been played on this ground, with the overall tally showing seven wins to England, and eight to Australia.

Matches here started in 1899, but it was not until 1956 that England managed a win. Six of the eight drawn Ashes Tests occurred before 1956, in conditions different from the modern era. Once they had broken their duck, England have prospered at Headingley. It is no coincidence that as conditions began to favour the bowlers, with the pitches accommodating seam bowling with variable bounce and overhead conditions helping swing, typical English pace bowlers came into their own. Australian batsmen, brought up on hard, fast pitches, found life more demanding. Nevertheless, in three of the last four Ashes Tests at Headingley, Australia won by 210 runs in 1989, an innings and 148 runs in 1993 and an innings and 61 runs in 1997. England had won four times in succession before that run, and in the most recent clash, in 2001, England enjoyed their only success of the series.

Sunset at Headingley Cricket Ground in Leeds, which will stage the fourth Ashes Test in 2009.

Fifth Test – The Oval, 20th–24th August

The Kennington Oval staged the first Test in England in 1880. It has since become the traditional venue for the final Test of a series, and consequently the scene of much history. England scraped home in 1880, losing five wickets while reaching 57, and have done particularly well in south London ever since. They have won 15 of the 34 Tests played there to Australia's six. Eight of the 13 draws have come in the 14 most recent matches, while Australia have won just twice since the war, in 1948 and 2001.

The draw in 2005 was akin to a win for England, because defeat would have resulted in the Ashes being retained by Australia. With a lead of only 133 when they lost their fifth wicket on the final day, England were facing that defeat. It was then that Pietersen compiled his first Test hundred with a blazing array of strokes at a time when the fate of the Ashes was in the balance. Pietersen's eighth-wicket partnership of 109 with Ashley Giles saw England to safety, with Australia's victory target of 342 no more than academic in deteriorating weather. Not even the anti-climactic ending, with the umpires deeming the light too bad for further

◀ Much has changed at Headingley, which stages both cricket and rugby, since this aerial photograph was taken of the ground in 1955.

play, could douse England's euphoria at winning the Ashes for the first time since 1987. Will there be such scenes again on the ground in 2009?

◀ An engraving of a match played at the Oval in 1881, in which W.G. Grace was one of the participants.

◀◀ The England squad during a training session at the Oval, 2007.

◄ The roof of the stand built for the 2005 Ashes series looms in the foreground at the Oval, where the final Test will be staged once again in 2009.

Other books also available:

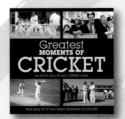
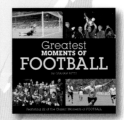

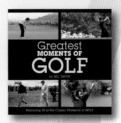

Available from all major stockists

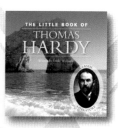

Available from all major stockists

The pictures in this book were provided courtesy of the following:

GETTY IMAGES
101 Bayham Street, London NW1 0AG

PA PHOTOS
www.paphotos.com

Creative Director: Kevin Gardner

Design and Artwork: David Wildish

Picture research: Ellie Charleston

Published by Green Umbrella Publishing

Publishers Jules Gammond and Vanessa Gardner

Written by Ralph Dellor and Stephen Lamb